One day Fergus woke up feeling strange. He looked at his reflection in the water and he was shocked to see that his whole body was multi-coloured.

Fergus hopped to where his brother Bob was sitting and he said, "Bob, I feel strange. I am multi-coloured and frogs are meant to be green!"

"Your feelings are all mixed up," said Bob, "Let me help you understand each feeling and you will feel much better."

Suddenly, Fergus turned yellow. "I feel fizzy and nervous," he said, "I am worried about what it will be like to learn about my feelings. I have a funny feeling in my tummy and my heart is beating fast."

"How you are feeling is ok Fergus," explained Bob. "Sometimes we can be worried or nervous and when we feel like this, talking to somebody can help."

"But frogs are meant to be green," whispered Fergus.

Just then a small fish jumped out of the water and splashed Fergus.

Fergus turned red.

"WATCH WHERE YOU JUMP!" screamed Fergus "I don't like being splashed!!"

I feel like I have a fire
in my belly….
IT'S NOT FAIR!" he
shouted as he jumped
up and down.

"You're feeling cross and angry,"
explained Bob. "When you feel like this it
is best to walk away or count to 10."

"I don't like this
feeling," said Fergus,
"frogs are meant to be
green!"

Tears started to run down Fergus' cheek and as they did, he turned blue.

"Frogs are meant to be green," sobbed Fergus, "and now I am blue. I am tired and sad and don't know what to do."

"Sadness does not feel nice," said Bob, "I will stay with you and help you to feel better."

"Thank you," said Fergus through his tears.

"Don't forget the party this afternoon." smiled Bob.

"Yippee!" cheered Fergus "I had forgotten about the party. I feel fizzy again but this time it's a good feeling. I am excited and I feel bouncy and happy!"

Bob said, "Yellow can also feel good fizzy. I am pleased you are happy again."

"Fizzy is a good feeling" said Fergus "but I know frogs are meant to be green."

That afternoon Fergus and Bob had a lovely time at the party. Fergus felt fizzy and bouncy and happy. He was yellow but he did not mind as he was having so much fun!

When Fergus woke up the next morning he thought " I feel ready for the day, whatever colour I am!"

He looked down at his reflection in the water and saw that he was green again.

As Fergus sat on his lily pad a smile appeared on his face.
"I feel calm, happy and confident. This must be what green feels like." he thought.

He sighed, "I know all my feelings are important and it is OK to feel each one from time to time, but I think I like green the best…….

...... after all, frogs are meant to be green!"

On the following pages you will find words you could use when talking about your feelings.

nervous
fearful
worried
delighted
excited
bouncy

unhappy
sad
gloomy
miserable
upset
down

bothered

angry

annoyed

livid

furious

cross

happy
calm
cool
peaceful
positive
relaxed

Printed in Great Britain
by Amazon

32288843R00021